The People of the Industrial Revolution
Elementary Supplement

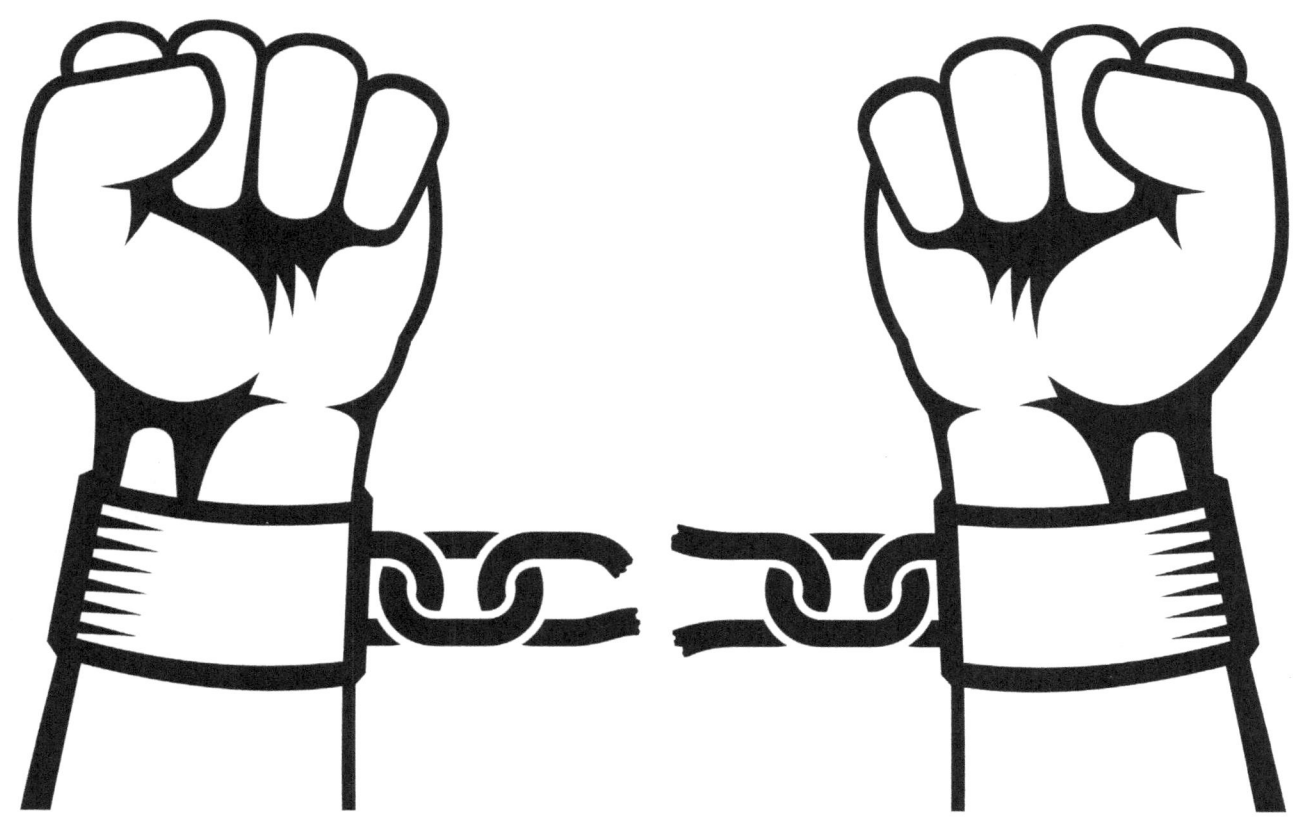

Fulton, KY

Current and upcoming titles:

Learn and Color Nature Series
- Medicinal Herbs
- Freshwater Fish
- Garden Edibles
- Reptiles

Learn and Color Stained Glass Series
- Landscapes & Seascapes
- Fish & Fowl
- Flowers

- Early Civilization
- The Ancient World
- The Middle Ages
- The Renaissance and Reformation
- The Industrial Revolution
- The Modern Age
- The Computer Age

Color Thru History™ – The People of the Industrial Revolution Elementary Supplement
© 2020 Master Design Marketing, LLC

All rights reserved. This book or parts thereof may not be reproduced in any form, stored in any retrieval system, or transmitted in any form by any means—electronic, mechanical, photocopy, recording, or otherwise—without prior written permission of the publisher, except as provided by United States of America copyright law or as noted below. For permission requests, write to the publisher, at "Permissions Coordinator," at the address below.

Learn & Color Books
 an imprint of Master Design Marketing, LLC
 789 State Route 94 E
 Fulton, KY 42041
 www.LearnAndColor.com

Permission is granted to make as many photocopies as you need for your own immediate family's homeschool use. All other use is strictly prohibited. Co-ops and schools may NOT photocopy any portion of this book. Educators must purchase one book for each student.

For information about special discounts available for bulk purchases, sales promotions, fund-raising and educational needs, contact Learn & Color Books at sales@LearnAndColor.com.

ISBN: 978-1-947482-28-9
Cover and interior design by Faithe F Thomas
Research by Caitlyn F Williams
Some images are © Faithe F Thomas
All other Images © DepositPhotos.com
Text in this book is a derivative of information by Wikipedia.com, used under CC BY 4.0.
The text of this book is licensed under CC BY 4.0 by Faithe F Thomas.
Look for the Scottish Flag somewhere in each of our books.

Benjamin Franklin was one of the Founding Fathers of the United States. Franklin was an author, printer, political theorist, politician, freemason, postmaster, scientist, inventor, humorist, statesman, and diplomat.

Saint Petersburg

Catherine the Great was Empress of Russia, the country's longest-ruling female leader. The period of her rule, the Catherinian Era, is considered the Golden Age of Russia.

George Washington was a Founding Father of the United States, who also served as the first President of the United States under the Constitution. He has been called the "Father of His Country."

James Watt was a Scottish inventor, mechanical engineer, and chemist who built a steam engine.

Johann Wolfgang von Goethe was a German writer and statesman.
He also created over 3,000 drawings.

Wolfgang Amadeus Mozart was a composer of the classical era.
He composed more than 600 works, including many famous pieces.

Eli Whitney was an American inventor.
Whitney is most famous for the cotton gin.
The cotton gin changed the way cotton was harvested

Napoléon Bonaparte was a French military leader during the French Revolution. He became Emperor of the French as Napoleon I.

Ludwig van Beethoven was a German composer and pianist.
He is one of the most recognized and influential of all composers.

Jane Austen was an English novelist. Her novels have inspired many films, from 1940's *Pride and Prejudice* to more recent productions.

Sacagawea was a Lemhi Shoshone Indian woman who is known for her help to the Lewis and Clark Expedition as they explored the Louisiana Territory.

Michael Faraday was a British scientist who studied electromagnetism. He was one of the most influential scientists in history.

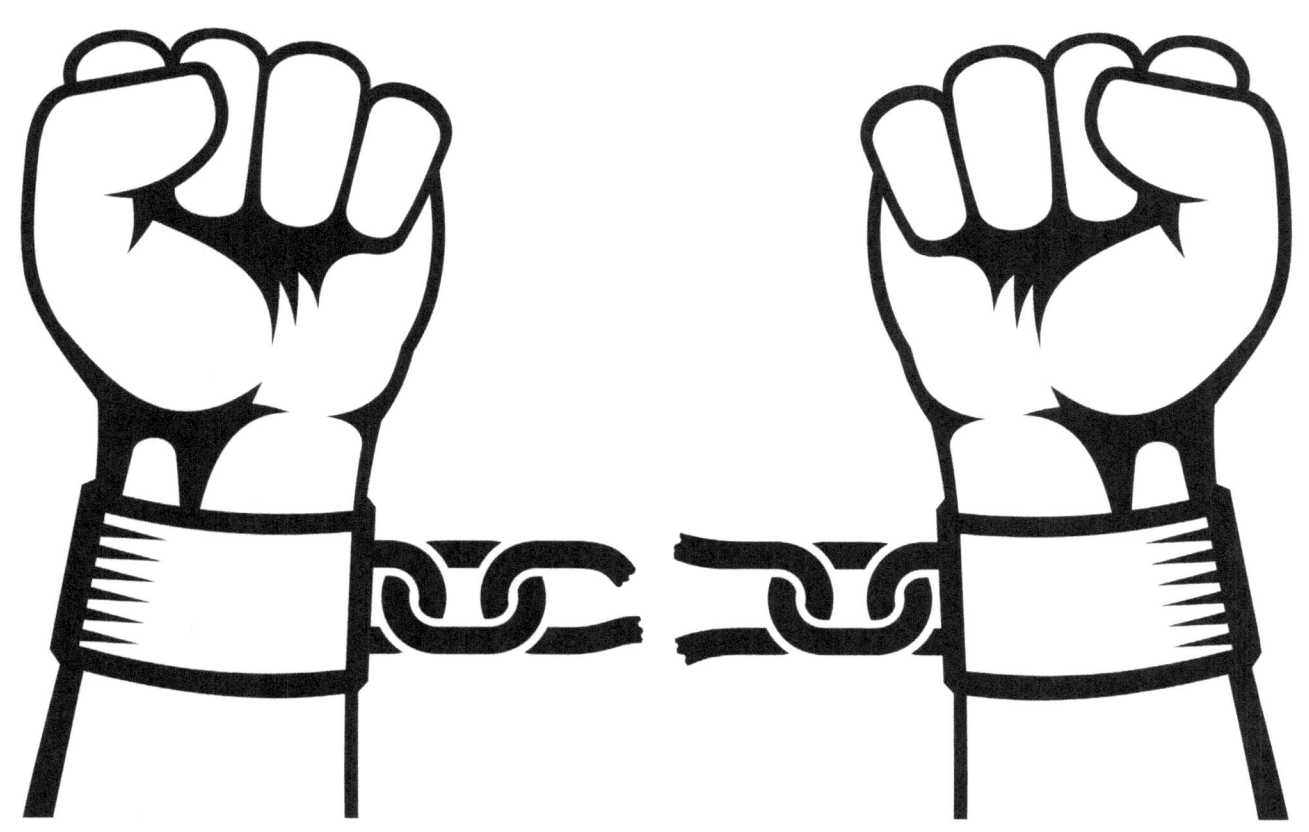

Sojourner Truth was a African-American woman who was born into slavery, but escaped with her infant daughter to freedom. She spoke out and demanded equal human rights for all women as well as for blacks.

Isambard Kingdom Brunel was an English engineer who built dockyards, the Great Western Railway, a series of steamships, and many important bridges and tunnels in England.

Abraham Lincoln was one of the greatest U.S. presidents.
He led the nation through the American Civil War.

Charles Robert Darwin was an English naturalist, geologist and biologist, best known for his theories of evolution.

Charles Dickens was an English writer.
He was the greatest novelist of the Victorian era.
He wrote *A Christmas Carol* and *A Tale of Two Cities*.

David Livingstone was a Protestant missionary to Africa, scientific investigator, explorer, imperial reformer, anti-slavery crusader, and advocate of commercial and colonial expansion.

Karl Marx was a German philosopher, economist, historian, sociologist, political theorist, journalist and socialist revolutionary.
His teachings are called socialism.

Queen Victoria reigned as queen of England for over 63 years. She had a very strict way of living. The time that she was queen is known as the Victorian Era.

Florence Nightingale was an English nurse and social reformer. The annual International Nurses Day is celebrated around the world on her birthday.

Susan B. Anthony was an American social reformer and women's rights activist who helped women get the right to vote.

Louis Pasteur was a French biologist known for inventing vaccinations and pasteurization.

Leo Tolstoy was a Russian writer. Many think he is one of the greatest authors of all time. He is best known for a very long book called *War and Peace*.

Claude Monet was a French painter known for his outside landscape paintings, including his lily ponds.

Alexander Graham Bell was a Scottish-born scientist, inventor, and engineer who invented the first practical telephone. He also founded the American Telephone & Telegraph Company (AT&T).

Thomas Alva Edison invented many things, including the record player, the motion picture camera, and the light bulb.

Vincent van Gogh was a Dutch painter who created over 2,100 artworks. He loved to use bright colors and painted pictures of flowers.

Nikola Tesla was a Serbian-American inventor, electrical engineer, and mechanical engineer known for the design of the modern electricity power system.

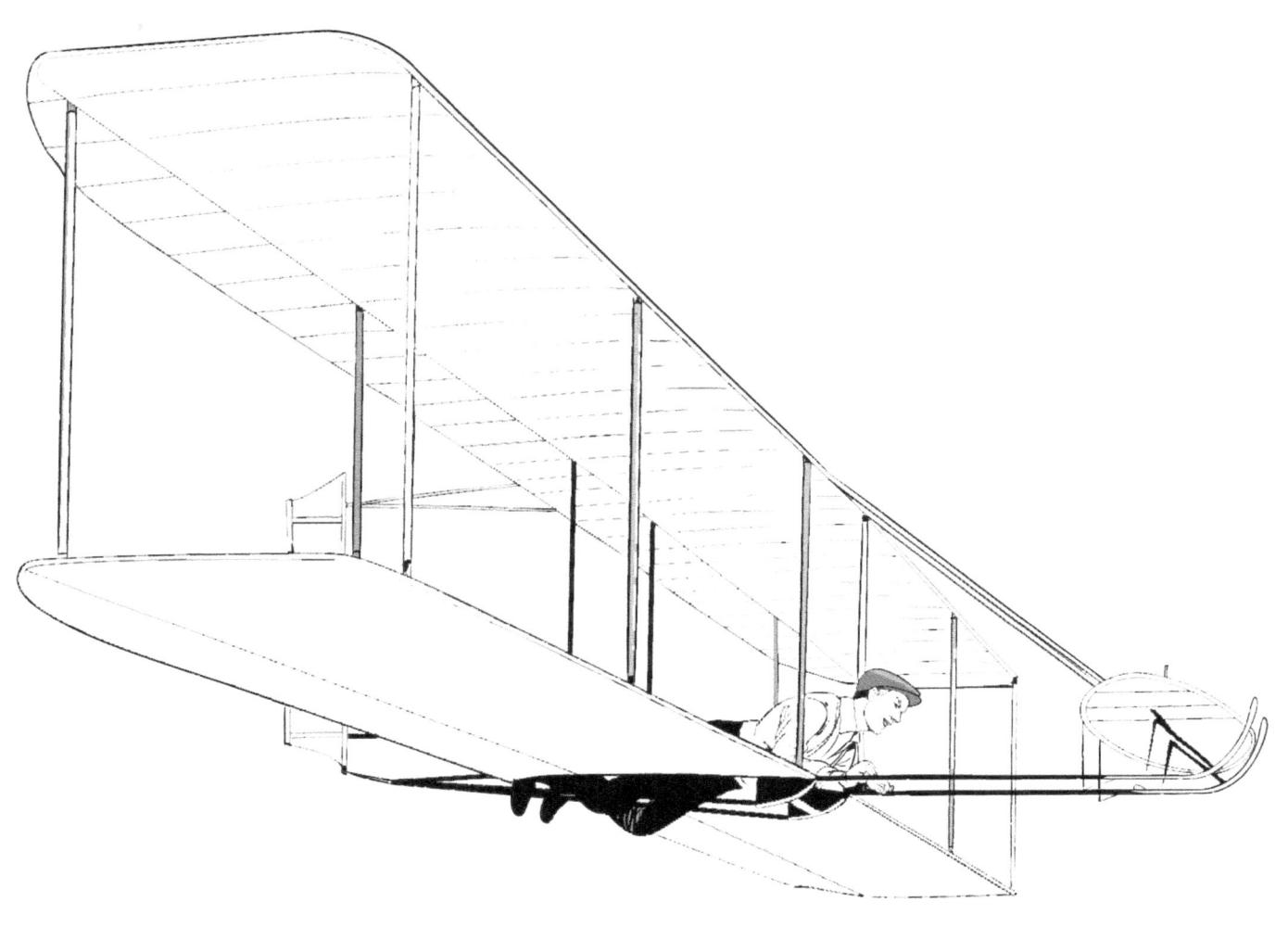

Orville Wright and Wilbur Wright, also known as the Wright brothers, were two American aviation pioneers generally credited with inventing, building, and flying the world's first successful airplane.